THE FAMILY PRAYERBOOK

Holidays and Festivals

SHELDON ZIMMERMAN

Illustrations by

ELEANOR SCHICK

Dallas, Texas

*For Judy, Brian, Kira,
David & Micol
and all the children and
families of Temple Emanu-El
S.Z.*

**The publication of this prayerbook is made
possible through the generosity of
Rhea Fay Fruhman,
the late Leo Fruhman,
and their son Leonard Fruhman**

Our gratitude to Seymour Rossel for his thoughtful, spiritual, and creative editing and guidance; and to Susan Salom for her caring help.

© Copyright 1988 by Temple Emanu-El of Dallas, Texas
All rights reserved.
ISBN 0-940646-60-9
*Distributed by
Behrman House, Inc.
235 Watchung Avenue
West Orange, NJ 07052*

HANUKKAH

Hanukkah is light and joy, gifts and good wishes. In this winter season when days are brief and nights are long, we join our people throughout the world, brightening the darkness with the candles and songs of Hanukkah.

בָּרְכוּ אֶת יְיָ הַמְבֹרָךְ.

Let us praise God.

בָּרוּךְ יְיָ הַמְבֹרָךְ לְעוֹלָם וָעֶד.

We praise God now and forever.

שְׁמַע יִשְׂרָאֵל: יְיָ אֱלֹהֵינוּ, יְיָ אֶחָד.

Hear, O Israel: The Lord is our God, the Lord is One.

בָּרוּךְ שֵׁם כְּבוֹד מַלְכוּתוֹ לְעוֹלָם וָעֶד.

Praised be God whose Rule is forever.

וְאָהַבְתָּ אֵת יְיָ אֱלֹהֶיךָ בְּכָל־לְבָבְךָ וּבְכָל־נַפְשְׁךָ וּבְכָל־מְאֹדֶךָ. וְהָיוּ הַדְּבָרִים הָאֵלֶּה, אֲשֶׁר אָנֹכִי מְצַוְּךָ הַיּוֹם, עַל־לְבָבֶךָ. וְשִׁנַּנְתָּם לְבָנֶיךָ. וְדִבַּרְתָּ בָּם בְּשִׁבְתְּךָ בְּבֵיתֶךָ, וּבְלֶכְתְּךָ בַדֶּרֶךְ וּבְשָׁכְבְּךָ וּבְקוּמֶךָ.

וּקְשַׁרְתָּם לְאוֹת עַל־יָדֶךָ, וְהָיוּ לְטֹטָפֹת בֵּין עֵינֶיךָ. וּכְתַבְתָּם עַל־מְזֻזוֹת בֵּיתֶךָ, וּבִשְׁעָרֶיךָ.

לְמַעַן תִּזְכְּרוּ וַעֲשִׂיתֶם אֶת־כָּל־מִצְוֹתָי, וִהְיִיתֶם קְדֹשִׁים לֵאלֹהֵיכֶם. אֲנִי יְיָ אֱלֹהֵיכֶם, אֲשֶׁר הוֹצֵאתִי אֶתְכֶם מֵאֶרֶץ מִצְרַיִם לִהְיוֹת לָכֶם לֵאלֹהִים. אֲנִי יְיָ אֱלֹהֵיכֶם.

You shall love *Adonai* your God
> **With all your strength and mind.**

These words which I command you today—
> **Keep them close to your heart.**

Teach them to your children,
> **Say them over and again.**

In the evening and in the morning,
> **Wherever you may be,**

When you speak, when you are silent,
> **Keep them close, very close.**

Copy these words;
> **Set them before you.**

On the doorposts of your homes,
> **And on your gates.**

So that you will remember your God
> **And do all of God's commandments,**

Today and every day of your life.

בָּרוּךְ אַתָּה, יְיָ, גָּאַל יִשְׂרָאֵל.

Baruch atah, Adonai,
> **We praise You, Adonai,**

Ga-al Yisrael,
> **For saving us,**

For helping us,
> **For giving us strength.**

Baruch atah, Adonai
> **Ga-al Yisrael.**

[A HANUKKAH SONG]

Our rabbis used a legend to explain Hanukkah: The day came when the Maccabees entered the Temple to rededicate it. To kindle the eternal light in the Temple menorah, they searched for oil blessed by the priests. At last, they found one small jar of oil . . . just enough for one day. They sent to the North for more oil, but they knew this would take many days. They did not wait. As the darkness came, they poured the oil from the small jar into the eternal light and set it aflame. When morning came, it was burning still. Then they gazed in wonder as night after night, day after day—for eight days, the oil still burned: one small light against the darkness.

ALL
This is the message of Hanukkah: the blackest darkness can be swept aside by even one small light, the wintry cold can be swept aside by one small flame.

Long ago, our people knew that in this season, the winter solstice, the long night rules over the day. The darkness frightens us, children and adults alike. Yet we know that this season will pass. Soon days will become longer and brighter again. In the same way, our sages said, the days of slavery and evil will pass. The day will come when all will be light and darkness and fear will vanish forever.

Until that day, they said, we must kindle lights. In the lights of Hanukkah we look forward to that day when all the world will be a place of beauty and peace.

ALL
On Hanukkah we thank God for helping the Maccabees win freedom for our people.

We tell again the story of the small jar of oil whose light drove back the shadows, and the story of the small band of warriors whose faith drove back the mighty armies of the North.

ALL
We remember that we are never too small to make a difference, our inner light is all the power we ever really need.

CANDLELIGHTING

בָּרוּךְ אַתָּה, יְיָ אֱלֹהֵינוּ, מֶלֶךְ הָעוֹלָם, אֲשֶׁר קִדְּשָׁנוּ בְּמִצְוֹתָיו, וְצִוָּנוּ לְהַדְלִיק נֵר שֶׁל חֲנֻכָּה.

Baruch atah, Adonai — **We praise You,** *Adonai* —
whose *mitzvot* **make us holy** —
for the *mitzvah* **of lighting and blessing**
the Hanukkah candles.

בָּרוּךְ אַתָּה, יְיָ אֱלֹהֵינוּ, מֶלֶךְ הָעוֹלָם, שֶׁעָשָׂה נִסִּים לַאֲבוֹתֵינוּ בַּיָּמִים הָהֵם בַּזְּמַן הַזֶּה.

Baruch atah, Adonai — We praise You, *Adonai*,
for all the wonderful things
You did for our ancestors
at this season long ago.

ON THE FIRST NIGHT ONLY

בָּרוּךְ אַתָּה, יְיָ אֱלֹהֵינוּ, מֶלֶךְ הָעוֹלָם,
שֶׁהֶחֱיָנוּ וְקִיְּמָנוּ וְהִגִּיעָנוּ לַזְּמַן הַזֶּה.

Baruch atah, Adonai — We praise You, *Adonai*,
for giving us life, health, and strength;
for parents and grandparents, children and friends;
for all our holidays; for Hanukkah;
for all Your many blessings and gifts,
we thank You, *Adonai*.

[A HANUKKAH SONG]

FOR GIFTS AND SHARING

On Hanukkah we receive gifts.
> **We receive many beautiful things:**

Toys and books, money and clothing.
> **We say "thank you."**

But there are those who do not receive presents.
> **They are poor and hungry; they need our help.**

We dedicate ourselves to bring them light,
> **To share with them our many blessings.**

We can make Hanukkah a time for sharing,
> **For sharing what we have with others.**

We rededicate ourselves as we once rededicated our Temple
> **We set an eternal light burning in our hearts,**

That the small lights of Hanukkah might last forever,
> **Until the day of peace when people everywhere will be free.**

SILENT PRAYER

CLOSING PRAYERS: PAGE 31

ROCK OF AGES

Rock of ages, let our song
    Praise Your saving power;
You, amid the raging foes,
    Were our sheltering tower.
Furious they assailed us,
    But Your arm availed us,
And Your word broke their sword,
    When our own strength failed us.

Kindling new the holy lamps,
    Priests approved in suffering,
Purified the nation's shrines,
    Brought to God their offering.
And God's courts surrounding
    Hear, in joy abounding,
Happy throngs, singing songs,
    With a mighty sounding.

Children of the Maccabees,
    Whether free or fettered,
Wake the echoes of the songs,
    Where you may be scattered.
Yours the message cheering,
    That the time is nearing,
Which will see all people free
    Tyrants disappearing.

PURIM

The rabbis set aside the whole month of Adar for joy and celebration. Purim is "our season of fun." On Purim, we boo Haman, cheer Mordecai and Esther, make noise with our *raashanim*, and celebrate with carnival merriment.

[A PURIM SONG]

Purim has its serious side, too. Many times, our people has faced enemies who meant to destroy us. Somehow we survived. We were saved by a Power greater than ourselves. On Purim we forge a link between frolic and solemnity. We celebrate the miracle and commemorate the mystery of Jewish survival.

Come then to joy. Come to say "thank you." Come and celebrate! We are here — we are alive! *Am Yisrael Chai!* We, the Jewish People, live and endure.

עַם יִשְׂרָאֵל חַי!

עוֹד אָבִינוּ חַי!

Am Yisrael Hai!

Od Avinu Hai!

We turn to God — Source of life and blessing — in rhapsody and joy, we come together as a community to pray.

בָּרְכוּ אֶת יְיָ הַמְבֹרָךְ.

Let us praise God.

בָּרוּךְ יְיָ הַמְבֹרָךְ לְעוֹלָם וָעֶד.

We praise God now and forever.

God has created a world of beauty and wonder.

We thank You, God, for our beautiful world.

God has created a world of orderliness and design.

We thank You, God, for bringing order to our world.

God called our people to Torah and *mitzvot*.

We thank You, God, for the Torah and for the *mitzvot* which add purpose to our lives.

For the Torah and *mitzvot*, for the world and its wonders, we praise You.
For Your love, which we feel every day, we thank You, God.

שְׁמַע יִשְׂרָאֵל: יְיָ אֱלֹהֵינוּ, יְיָ אֶחָד.

Hear, O Israel: The Lord is our God, the Lord is One.

בָּרוּךְ שֵׁם כְּבוֹד מַלְכוּתוֹ לְעוֹלָם וָעֶד.

Praised be God whose Rule is forever.

וְאָהַבְתָּ אֵת יְיָ אֱלֹהֶיךָ בְּכָל־לְבָבְךָ וּבְכָל־נַפְשְׁךָ וּבְכָל־מְאֹדֶךָ. וְהָיוּ הַדְּבָרִים הָאֵלֶּה, אֲשֶׁר אָנֹכִי מְצַוְּךָ הַיּוֹם, עַל־לְבָבֶךָ. וְשִׁנַּנְתָּם לְבָנֶיךָ. וְדִבַּרְתָּ בָּם בְּשִׁבְתְּךָ בְּבֵיתֶךָ, וּבְלֶכְתְּךָ בַדֶּרֶךְ וּבְשָׁכְבְּךָ וּבְקוּמֶךָ.

וּקְשַׁרְתָּם לְאוֹת עַל־יָדֶךָ, וְהָיוּ לְטֹטָפֹת בֵּין עֵינֶיךָ. וּכְתַבְתָּם עַל־מְזֻזוֹת בֵּיתֶךָ, וּבִשְׁעָרֶיךָ.

לְמַעַן תִּזְכְּרוּ וַעֲשִׂיתֶם אֶת־כָּל־מִצְוֹתָי, וִהְיִיתֶם קְדֹשִׁים לֵאלֹהֵיכֶם. אֲנִי יְיָ אֱלֹהֵיכֶם, אֲשֶׁר הוֹצֵאתִי אֶתְכֶם מֵאֶרֶץ מִצְרַיִם לִהְיוֹת לָכֶם לֵאלֹהִים. אֲנִי יְיָ אֱלֹהֵיכֶם.

You shall love *Adonai* your God
  With all your strength and mind.
These words which I command you today —
  Keep them close to your heart.
Teach them to your children,
  Say them over and again.
In the evening and in the morning,
  Wherever you may be,
When you speak, when you are silent,
  Keep them close, very close.
Copy these words;
  Set them before you.
On the doorposts of your homes,
  And on your gates.

So that you will remember your God
> **And do all of God's commandments,**
Today and every day of your life.

בָּרוּךְ אַתָּה, יְיָ, גָּאַל יִשְׂרָאֵל.

You saved us from Egypt many years ago. Again and again, You have been there for us. On Purim we remember the time, thousands of years ago, when Haman plotted to destroy us. Miraculously, Mordecai and Esther stopped him. Though Your name is not mentioned in the Scroll of Esther, we believe You were there, too. We praise You, O God, *Ga-al Yisrael* — Redeemer of Israel in the past. We praise You, O God, *Go-el Yisrael* — our Redeemer today, tomorrow, forever.

MEGILLAH BLESSINGS

בָּרוּךְ אַתָּה, יְיָ אֱלֹהֵינוּ, מֶלֶךְ הָעוֹלָם, אֲשֶׁר קִדְּשָׁנוּ בְּמִצְוֹתָיו, וְצִוָּנוּ עַל־מִקְרָא מְגִלָּה.

Blessed is *Adonai*, our God, Ruler of the universe —
whose *mitzvot* make us holy —
for the *mitzvah* of reading the *Megillah*.

בָּרוּךְ אַתָּה, יְיָ אֱלֹהֵינוּ, מֶלֶךְ הָעוֹלָם, שֶׁעָשָׂה נִסִּים לַאֲבוֹתֵינוּ בַּיָּמִים הָהֵם בַּזְּמַן הַזֶּה.

Blessed is *Adonai* our God, Ruler of the universe,
who performed wondrous deeds for our ancestors
many years ago at this season.

בָּרוּךְ אַתָּה, יְיָ אֱלֹהֵינוּ, מֶלֶךְ הָעוֹלָם, שֶׁהֶחֱיָנוּ וְקִיְּמָנוּ וְהִגִּיעָנוּ לַזְּמַן הַזֶּה.

Blessed is *Adonai* our God, Ruler of the universe,
for giving us life, providing for us,
and bringing us to this festive day.

The *Megillah* tells an old story. The Persian Prime Minister, Haman, tried to destroy our people. He told King Ahasuerus that the Jewish people were evil and had to be killed. It took great courage for Queen Esther to stop Haman from carrying out his evil plan.

As we read the *Megillah*, we are inspired by Esther's bravery and the wisdom of her uncle Mordecai. In many times and places, other Hamans have arisen to destroy our people. With wisdom and courage, and with God's help, we have survived.

As we read the *Megillah*, let us remember its lesson. Together, prayer and action make a mighty team. Our prayers bring us wisdom, even as our actions unite us.

READING OF THE MEGILLAH

CLOSING HYMN

AND

PROCESSIONAL IN COSTUMES

PASSOVER

At this season, our people sit at *Seder* tables telling the story of Passover, eating the Passover meal, and singing songs of freedom. With family and friends we remember that ancient time when we were freed from slavery. We recite four questions, just as we have done throughout the ages.

Mah nishtanah halayla hazeh mikol halelot.
    "*Mah nishtanah*," we ask, "Why is this night different?"
On all other nights we eat all kinds of bread;
    Tonight we eat only *matzah*.
On all other nights we eat all kinds of vegetables;
    Tonight we eat *maror*, bitter herbs.
On all other nights we do not dip our foods;
    Tonight we dip twice — in salt water and in *haroset*.
On all other nights we eat quickly
    Sometimes sitting, sometimes standing.
We eat quickly: sometimes alone, sometimes together.
    Tonight we eat slowly, together as families,
Leaning back against the cushions in our chairs.
    Remembering and retelling the story of freedom.

ALL

מַה־נִּשְׁתַּנָּה הַלַּיְלָה הַזֶּה מִכָּל־הַלֵּילוֹת.

שֶׁבְּכָל־הַלֵּילוֹת אָנוּ אוֹכְלִין חָמֵץ וּמַצָּה.
הַלַּיְלָה הַזֶּה כֻּלּוֹ מַצָּה.

שֶׁבְּכָל־הַלֵּילוֹת אָנוּ אוֹכְלִין שְׁאָר יְרָקוֹת.
הַלַּיְלָה הַזֶּה מָרוֹר.

שֶׁבְּכָל־הַלֵּילוֹת אָנוּ מַטְבִּילִין אֲפִלּוּ פַּעַם אֶחָת.
הַלַּיְלָה הַזֶּה שְׁתֵּי פְעָמִים.

שֶׁבְּכָל־הַלֵּילוֹת אָנוּ אוֹכְלִין בֵּין יוֹשְׁבִין וּבֵין מְסֻבִּין.
הַלַּיְלָה הַזֶּה כֻּלָּנוּ מְסֻבִּין.

This is our story, the *Maggid* — the story of our people and our God. The *Seder* night is different. Passover is unique among the holidays.

בָּרְכוּ אֶת יְיָ הַמְבֹרָךְ.
Let us praise God.

בָּרוּךְ יְיָ הַמְבֹרָךְ לְעוֹלָם וָעֶד.
We praise God now and forever.

Mah nishtanah, why is this holiday different?

ALL

We remember an ancient time: Each year, in the spring, when the new lambs were born, our people sacrificed a lamb. They called this lamb, the *pesach*. They thanked God for their flocks of sheep, for God's love for their fathers and mothers — Abraham and Sarah, Isaac and Rebecca, Jacob, Leah, and Rachel. Today, we remember their *pesach*, the special lamb sacrifice, and their love and devotion to God. May our hearts be turned to God. May we always love God, as God has always loved our people. May we learn to love God as God loves us.

שְׁמַע יִשְׂרָאֵל: יְיָ אֱלֹהֵינוּ, יְיָ אֶחָד.
Hear, O Israel: The Lord is our God, the Lord is One.

בָּרוּךְ שֵׁם כְּבוֹד מַלְכוּתוֹ לְעוֹלָם וָעֶד.
Praised be God whose Rule is forever.

וְאָהַבְתָּ אֵת יְיָ אֱלֹהֶיךָ בְּכָל־לְבָבְךָ וּבְכָל־נַפְשְׁךָ וּבְכָל־מְאֹדֶךָ. וְהָיוּ הַדְּבָרִים הָאֵלֶּה, אֲשֶׁר אָנֹכִי מְצַוְּךָ הַיּוֹם, עַל־לְבָבֶךָ. וְשִׁנַּנְתָּם לְבָנֶיךָ. וְדִבַּרְתָּ בָּם בְּשִׁבְתְּךָ בְּבֵיתֶךָ. וּבְלֶכְתְּךָ בַדֶּרֶךְ וּבְשָׁכְבְּךָ וּבְקוּמֶךָ.

וּקְשַׁרְתָּם לְאוֹת עַל־יָדֶךָ. וְהָיוּ לְטֹטָפֹת בֵּין עֵינֶיךָ. וּכְתַבְתָּם עַל־מְזֻזוֹת בֵּיתֶךָ. וּבִשְׁעָרֶיךָ.

לְמַעַן תִּזְכְּרוּ וַעֲשִׂיתֶם אֶת־כָּל־מִצְוֹתָי. וִהְיִיתֶם קְדֹשִׁים לֵאלֹהֵיכֶם.

אֲנִי יְיָ אֱלֹהֵיכֶם, אֲשֶׁר הוֹצֵאתִי אֶתְכֶם מֵאֶרֶץ מִצְרַיִם לִהְיוֹת לָכֶם לֵאלֹהִים. אֲנִי יְיָ אֱלֹהֵיכֶם.

You shall love *Adonai* your God
   With all your strength and mind.
These words which I command you today —
   Keep them close to your heart.
Teach them to your children,
   Say them over and again.
In the evening and in the morning,
   Wherever you may be,
When you speak, when you are silent,
   Keep them close, very close.
Copy these words;
   Set them before you.
On the doorposts of your homes,
   And on your gates.
So that you will remember your God
   And do all of God's commandments,
Today and every day of your life.

ALL

Mah nishtanah, **Why is this holiday different?**

We remember an ancient time: Our people were slaves to Pharaoh. They came down to Egypt to live with Joseph, bringing their flocks in a joyous procession. For many years they lived in freedom until a new Pharaoh was crowned who did not remember Joseph and the wonderful things Joseph had done for Egypt and all the Egyptians. Then Pharaoh took away our freedom and forced us to serve as slaves.

[A PASSOVER SONG]

With toil and tears we made bricks,
   In pain and sadness, we built the Pharaoh's cities.
We suffered the whip of the Pharaoh's taskmasters.
   We asked, "Has God forgotten us?"

"Has God forgotten the promises made
> **"To our mothers and our fathers,**

"To give their children the land of Israel,
> **"As their inheritance forever?"**

But God did not forget. God set our people free. With mighty acts, with great power, God set us free — free to worship God in the wilderness, free to enter the promised land, the land of Israel, the land of hope and freedom. Slaves no more, we sang a new song, a song of praise to God who saved us.

מִי־כָמֹכָה בָּאֵלִם, יְיָ?

מִי כָּמֹכָה, נֶאְדָּר בַּקֹּדֶשׁ, נוֹרָא תְהִלֹּת, עֹשֵׂה פֶלֶא?

מַלְכוּתְךָ רָאוּ בָנֶיךָ בּוֹקֵעַ יָם לִפְנֵי מֹשֶׁה:

"זֶה אֵלִי!" עָנוּ וְאָמְרוּ: "יְיָ יִמְלֹךְ לְעֹלָם וָעֶד!"

ALL
Mah nishtanah, **Why is this holiday different?**

We remember a time soon after Egyptian slavery. Our people were farmers in Canaan, the Promised Land. They remembered the *pesach*, the ancient sacrifice. They remembered Egypt and the tears and trials of slavery. How they danced when God saved them! How they laughed and sang for the greening of the land in the spring! Once again they brought the *pesach*, the lamb sacrifice. And, as they ate, they spoke of how slavery turned to freedom, how darkness turned to light, how sadness turned to joy.

Me-avdut le-cherut. "From slavery to freedom."
> **They prayed and sang through the night.**

They thanked God for the earth and the springtime; for all that lives and grows.
> **They made bread from the grain of their early spring harvest,**

Matzah, unleavened bread, to remind them of Egypt:
> **When they left so quickly their bread had no time to rise,**

Carried on their backs, the dough baked dry and flat in the heat of the desert sun.
> **Just like the *matzah* they were eating, and the *matzah* we eat today.**

[A PASSOVER SONG]

ALL

With the *matzah* and the *pesach* and the *maror* — the bitter herbs — they told their story: how God saved them from Egypt and Pharaoh, from slavery and bondage, so many years before.

After the Temple was destroyed, our people could no longer bring the *pesach* offering, but they ate *matzah* and *maror* and told how God rescued us. They sang songs of freedom and paeans of praise. They made Passover a night of remembering. They ordained a great feast, giving it an order, a "*seder*," in their book of memories, the *Haggadah*.

אֵלִיָּהוּ הַנָּבִיא, אֵלִיָּהוּ הַתִּשְׁבִּי,
אֵלִיָּהוּ, אֵלִיָּהוּ, אֵלִיָּהוּ הַגִּלְעָדִי.
בִּמְהֵרָה בְיָמֵינוּ, יָבֹא אֵלֵינוּ,
עִם מָשִׁיחַ בֶּן דָּוִד, עִם מָשִׁיחַ בֶּן דָּוִד.

Eliyahu Hanavi, Eliyahu Hatishbi
Eliyahu, Eliyahu, Eliyahu Hagiladi
Bimheira, viyameinu, yavo aleinu,
Im Mashiach ben David, im Mashiach ben David.

Mah nishtanah,
   Why is this holiday different?
Because the story never ends.
   Our people still lives, proof that God never forgets.
Proof that God always remembers the ancient promise
   That one day soon all Jews will be free.
That one day soon people everywhere will be free.
   So the legend tells: That in every home,
Eliyahu hanavi, Elijah the prophet
   Visits the seder and joins every family,
Blesses every child as he sips one sip of wine.
   So we, too, remember the promise.

We, too, pray for that day to come
> **When all Jews will be free wherever they may live,**

When Israel will be safe and secure in peace and in joy.
> **When all God's children will be free.**

Free to dream, to sing, and to love.
> **When all God's children will know peace and blessing forever.**

SILENT PRAYER

CLOSING PRAYERS: PAGE 31

CLOSING HYMN

SHAVUOT
The Fruits of our Harvest

"How good it is and how pleasant when people come together in friendship."

הִנֵּה מַה־טּוֹב וּמַה־נָּעִים, שֶׁבֶת אַחִים גַּם־יָחַד.

Hinei ma tov umana-im, shevet achim gam yachad.

ALL
How good it is to come together: to sing, to pray, to thank God. How good it is to come together: young and old, children and parents, grandparents and family. How good it is to come together: to sing, to pray, to offer thanks to our God.

בָּרְכוּ אֶת יְיָ הַמְבֹרָךְ.
Let us praise God.

בָּרוּךְ יְיָ הַמְבֹרָךְ לְעוֹלָם וָעֶד.
We praise God now and forever.

Thank You for the beauty around us,
   Trees, flowers, and earth.
Thank You for the radiance around us,
   Sun, moon, and stars.
Thank You for the majesty around us.
   Thank You, God, for the gift of Your creation:
For parents, grandparents, and friends.
   Thank You, God.
For Torah and *mitzvot*,
   Thank You, God.
For our congregation and all it teaches us,
   We give thanks to You, O God.

שְׁמַע יִשְׂרָאֵל: יְיָ אֱלֹהֵינוּ, יְיָ אֶחָד.
Hear, O Israel: The Lord is our God, the Lord is One.

בָּרוּךְ שֵׁם כְּבוֹד מַלְכוּתוֹ לְעוֹלָם וָעֶד.
Praised be God whose Rule is forever.

וְאָהַבְתָּ אֵת יְיָ אֱלֹהֶיךָ בְּכָל־לְבָבְךָ וּבְכָל־נַפְשְׁךָ וּבְכָל־מְאֹדֶךָ. וְהָיוּ הַדְּבָרִים הָאֵלֶּה. אֲשֶׁר אָנֹכִי מְצַוְּךָ הַיּוֹם. עַל־לְבָבֶךָ. וְשִׁנַּנְתָּם לְבָנֶיךָ. וְדִבַּרְתָּ בָּם בְּשִׁבְתְּךָ בְּבֵיתֶךָ. וּבְלֶכְתְּךָ בַדֶּרֶךְ וּבְשָׁכְבְּךָ וּבְקוּמֶךָ.

וּקְשַׁרְתָּם לְאוֹת עַל־יָדֶךָ. וְהָיוּ לְטֹטָפֹת בֵּין עֵינֶיךָ. וּכְתַבְתָּם עַל־מְזֻזוֹת בֵּיתֶךָ. וּבִשְׁעָרֶיךָ.

לְמַעַן תִּזְכְּרוּ וַעֲשִׂיתֶם אֶת־כָּל־מִצְוֹתָי. וִהְיִיתֶם קְדֹשִׁים לֵאלֹהֵיכֶם. אֲנִי יְיָ אֱלֹהֵיכֶם. אֲשֶׁר הוֹצֵאתִי אֶתְכֶם מֵאֶרֶץ מִצְרַיִם לִהְיוֹת לָכֶם לֵאלֹהִים. אֲנִי יְיָ אֱלֹהֵיכֶם.

You shall love *Adonai* your God
   With all your strength and mind.
These words which I command you today—
   Keep them close to your heart.
Teach them to your children,
   Say them over and again.
In the evening and in the morning,
   Wherever you may be,
When you speak, when you are silent,
   Keep them close, very close.
Copy these words;
   Set them before you.
On the doorposts of your homes,
   And on your gates.
So that you will remember your God
   And do all of God's commandments,
Today and every day of your life.

This Holy Day is our festival of Shavuot. It is also called the holiday of "Weeks" for we celebrate it seven weeks to the day after Passover begins. And we call it "the time of the giving of Our Torah." On a Shavuot not so long ago, our ancestors stood at the foot of Mt. Sinai to receive the Torah. On Shavuot the Torah was given. Later, in the land of Israel, our people came to the Temple on Shavuot to thank God for the Torah. They brought offerings from their early summer harvest, the *bikkurim*: the first fruits, the wheat, and the flowers. Today we bring our children, the fruits of our harvest, to be blessed before God and our congregation.

PARENTS BRINGING BABIES BORN IN THE PAST
YEAR ARE CALLED UP TO THE HOLY ARK

THE ARK IS OPENED

PARENTS

As our ancestors made their sacred pilgrimage to Jerusalem they carried the first fruits of their harvest. In grateful recollection of their faithfulness and in keeping with the ancient tradition of *bikkurim* we gather to give thanks, bringing our children, the symbol of our many blessings. May God's blessings be theirs and ours throughout life.

בָּרוּךְ אַתָּה, יְיָ אֱלֹהֵינוּ, מֶלֶךְ הָעוֹלָם.
שֶׁהֶחֱיָנוּ וְקִיְּמָנוּ וְהִגִּיעָנוּ לַזְּמַן הַזֶּה.

Baruch atah, Adonai, Elohenu melech ha-olam
Shehecheyanu v'kimanu v'higianu lazman hazeh.

Thank You, God, for giving us life and strength,
and helping us reach this moment of joy and blessing.
Amen.

[THE RABBI BLESSES PARENTS AND CHILDREN]

ALL

As our ancestors stood at Sinai on this holy day and heard God's words, so do we hear them again. O God, grant us and grant our children courage and wisdom, that we and they may remain faithful to You and Your Torah forever.

[A SHAVUOT SONG]

THE TEN COMMANDMENTS

[1]
I, the Highest, am your God who led you out of the land of Egypt, out of the house of bondage.

[2]
You shall have no other Gods beside Me. You shall not worship images of anything in the heavens, the earth, or the waters.

I, the Highest, your God, require loyalty from you and your children forever. I remember for a few generations those who are disloyal.

But I show steadfast love for thousands of generations to those who love Me and keep My commandments.

[3]
You shall not invoke the name of the Highest, your God, with malice.

[4]
Remember the sabbath day and keep it holy. Six days shall you labor and do all your work, but the seventh day is a sabbath of the Lord your God:

You shall do no work—you, your son or daughter, your servants, your domestic animals, or the stranger in your community.

For in six days the Highest One made heaven and earth, the sea, and all that is in them; then God rested on the seventh day. Therefore, the Lord blessed the sabbath and called it holy.

[5]
Honor your father and your mother, that you may long endure in the land that the Highest, your God, gives to you.

[6]
You shall not murder.

[7]
You shall not commit adultery.

[8]
You shall not steal.

[9]
You shall not bear false witness against your neighbor.

[10]
You shall not covet your neighbor's house, your neighbor's wife, nor his servants, nor his cattle, nor anything that is your neighbor's.

SILENT PRAYER

CLOSING PRAYERS: PAGE 30

ALL

שָׁלוֹם חַבֵרִים, לְהִתְרָאוֹת.

Shalom Chaverim
Shalom chaverim, shalom chaverim
Shalom, shalom
L'hitra-ot, l'hitra-ot,
Shalom, shalom.

Shalom everyone, shalom everyone
Shalom to you.
We're glad that you've come
For friendship and fun
May God bless you.

CLOSING PRAYERS

ADORATION

עָלֵינוּ לְשַׁבֵּחַ לַאֲדוֹן הַכֹּל. לָתֵת גְּדֻלָּה לְיוֹצֵר בְּרֵאשִׁית.
שֶׁלֹּא עָשָׂנוּ כְּגוֹיֵי הָאֲרָצוֹת. וְלֹא שָׂמָנוּ כְּמִשְׁפְּחוֹת הָאֲדָמָה:
שֶׁלֹּא שָׂם חֶלְקֵנוּ כָּהֶם. וְגֹרָלֵנוּ כְּכָל־הֲמוֹנָם.

Let us adore the everliving God
    And render praise unto *Adonai*
Who spread out the Heavens and established the earth
    Whose glory is revealed in the Heavens above
And whose greatness is manifest throughout the world
    Adonai is our God, there is none else

וַאֲנַחְנוּ כֹּרְעִים וּמִשְׁתַּחֲוִים וּמוֹדִים
לִפְנֵי מֶלֶךְ מַלְכֵי הַמְּלָכִים. הַקָּדוֹשׁ בָּרוּךְ הוּא.

Va-a-nach-nu Ko-r'im U-mish-ta-cha-vim U-mo-dim
    Lif-nei Me-lech Mal-chei Ham-la-chim
        Ha-ka-dosh Ba-ruch Hu

We bow the head in reverence
    And worship *Adonai* our God,
The Holy One, *Hakadosh*.

בַּיּוֹם הַהוּא יִהְיֶה יְיָ אֶחָד וּשְׁמוֹ אֶחָד.

Bayom hahu, bayom hahu yihyeh Adonai echad u'shmo echad.

On that day God shall be One,
    And God's name shall be One.

KADDISH

יִתְגַּדַּל וְיִתְקַדַּשׁ שְׁמֵהּ רַבָּא בְּעָלְמָא דִּי־בְרָא כִרְעוּתֵהּ.
וְיַמְלִיךְ מַלְכוּתֵהּ בְּחַיֵּיכוֹן וּבְיוֹמֵיכוֹן וּבְחַיֵּי דְכָל־בֵּית יִשְׂרָאֵל.
בַּעֲגָלָא וּבִזְמַן קָרִיב. וְאִמְרוּ: אָמֵן.
יְהֵא שְׁמֵהּ רַבָּא מְבָרַךְ לְעָלַם וּלְעָלְמֵי עָלְמַיָּא.
יִתְבָּרַךְ וְיִשְׁתַּבַּח. וְיִתְפָּאַר וְיִתְרוֹמַם וְיִתְנַשֵּׂא. וְיִתְהַדָּר וְיִתְעַלֶּה
וְיִתְהַלָּל שְׁמֵהּ דְּקוּדְשָׁא. בְּרִיךְ הוּא. לְעֵלָּא מִן־כָּל־בִּרְכָתָא
וְשִׁירָתָא. תֻּשְׁבְּחָתָא וְנֶחֱמָתָא דַּאֲמִירָן בְּעָלְמָא. וְאִמְרוּ: אָמֵן.
יְהֵא שְׁלָמָא רַבָּא מִן־שְׁמַיָּא וְחַיִּים עָלֵינוּ וְעַל־כָּל־יִשְׂרָאֵל. וְאִמְרוּ: אָמֵן.

Raise high and glorify the name of God
    Throughout the world God chose to create.
May God's kingdom be built
    In your lifetime, during your days,
And in the lifetime of all the House of Israel,
    Soon, and in a time close at hand.
So let us say, Amen.

Let the name of the Holy One, the Blessed,
    Be praised and glorified,
Be exalted, raised up and honored,
    Be magnified and spread.
Though we know God is above all praises,
    Above all songs of praise, and above all blessings,
Above all kind words we speak in our world,
    Even so, we say, Amen.

Let peace pour from the heavens
    With life for us and for all Israel.
So let us say, Amen.

עֹשֶׂה שָׁלוֹם בִּמְרוֹמָיו. הוּא יַעֲשֶׂה שָׁלוֹם
עָלֵינוּ וְעַל־כָּל־יִשְׂרָאֵל. וְאִמְרוּ: אָמֵן.

Creator of peace in the highest places,
    May God create peace for us and for all Israel.
For this, we say, Amen.